The Sex Kind Of Love

Amazing Approach To Optimizing Sex In A Relationship

By Alma J. Reese

Table of contents

Chapter 1

Introduction

Rarely does a relationship go through life without some difficulties?
You will have a lot more success moving beyond any potential relationship issues if you are aware of them in advance.

Successful couples have learned how to deal with the hiccups and maintain their love life even though every relationship has its ups and downs.
They persevere, confront concerns, and develop the skills necessary to resolve the challenging situations encountered in daily life.

Many people achieve this by reading self-help books and articles, going to seminars, getting therapy, looking at other happy couples, or just winging it.
Long-term relationships are particularly difficult. There are so many things that may go wrong in a relationship that is often difficult to fix. Yes, you should sit down and speak things out, spend some time apart from each other, or maybe look into getting help from a couple's therapist.

More issues develop when couples use sex to hide their emotional difficulties and don't participate in talking what is happening between them, then the sex works in reverse, It separates you.

Even worse, you created a risky trend. It may become somewhat addicting to use sex as a way to avoid engaging in emotional closeness via communication and presence.

Your troubles won't all be solved by sex, but it may assist with some of them.

It's excellent news, then! Who needs to pay for couples therapy or spend all night fighting in the kitchen? Just schedule some alone time with your significant other and resolve the issue in bed. (Or is it higher? Or avoid going there.) The problem is that you can't use it as a substitute for putting in the effort necessary to make a relationship succeed.

Chapter 2

Relationship issues that sex may truly help with

1 You two don't spend enough time together;

People sometimes struggle to find time to spend with their partners because of their hectic schedules. It may not seem seductive at all to schedule sex, but it should be done in the worst situation. Make a date night that entails remaining in and being intimate rather than having to drag your exhausted selves to a restaurant (and argue over which one). No pressure, of course, but it will assist if you at least place yourself in a setting and state of mind that supports sex.

2 When you aren't conversing with one another;

Your lover sees more of you thanks to sex. Make getting laid out a top priority if you feel like you're simply not conversing anymore. Physical contact is a terrific method to remove the barriers that might exist between a couple and get to the root of the problem. I often discover that after having fantastic sex, we are much more honest and intelligent than when we merely argue about who has the right, to tell the truth. That seems reasonable. After the act, set aside some time to relax and have fun with each other.

3 When you need to push the reset button;

Even the finest partnerships may have uninteresting sexual encounters sometimes, and for some couples, this unhappiness is the major issue. Most couples ultimately cope with it.

The depressing reality about sex is this: In many long-term relationships, it serves as either the bonding agent that binds things together or the cause of ongoing suffering and strife. You simply need to have more sex with your lover if it sounds similar. Nevertheless better sex.

It could be awkward to discuss what's wrong with your relationship, but you'll have to. Remember the three G's for a good sex life: being Good, Giving, and Game in the bedroom. Don't do anything you don't want to.

4 Whenever you need to reconcile after a dispute;

The greatest way to apologize is really to have sex. Because we engage in makeup sex while fully conscious of the emotional substance of the disputes we must address, that it is highly heated. Makeup sex may be quite sensual. So instead of fighting, bang each other when you find yourself in conflict. After that, maturely discuss your issues and find a solution. Sometimes, it's a bit simpler to acknowledge you're incorrect thanks to the sex.

5 strengthens your relationship with your partner;

Sex is just one aspect of intimacy. The steps leading to the bedroom are all equally significant. Relationships also require elements like physical attractiveness and passion for your partner. These physical interactions—touching, holding hands, and exchanging kisses—remind you that you do, in fact, like one another.

6 Encourages you to schedule time for one another;

Physical intimacy is impossible while you are separated. You are in the same location at the same time, enjoying one another whether it is planned or unplanned. Intimacy often falls to the bottom of the list of priorities when spouses are busy with their work and having children. When you're together, you've blocked out everything else and are only with one another.

7 Allows you to temporarily put your worries about the world aside;

Many of the issues we have in our relationships may result from the stress we let enter our lives from other sources. If we aren't cautious, our aspirations of pleasure in our jobs, families, and personal lives might take precedence and keep us apart from our partners. When done well, intimacy encourages you to keep your attention entirely on your companion.

8 Offers a space for creativity, vulnerability, and restraint;

It may be liberating to be intimate with someone you love and trust. In those private times with your lover, you are free to act and behave as you choose. In that bedroom, you are free to be as imaginative, kooky, and fun as you choose.

Sex is beneficial for relationships between couples. It may be soothing, restorative, and even calorie-burning. No, it won't fix all of your relationship issues, but it will provide advantages that help you and your spouse reach a healthy, secure, and happy position in your relationship. Make sure to look for practical and targeted answers to your problems in the front end. And only utilize closeness in your relationship for the pleasure it was intended for.

Don't be scared to utilize sex as a coping mechanism for certain issues. Just make sure you're addressing the issues and feeling like you're receiving what you need out of the bedroom and back in.

Chapter 3

Relationship issues that sex alone can not help with:

There is nothing better than a hair-pulling, dirty-talking, sweating session in the covers with your significant other to shake off a bad day if you are in a loving, devoted relationship. There are benefits to using sex as a stress reliever. But when you use sex to "fix" issues in your relationship or your life that call for genuine thinking, time, effort, and solutions, you get into trouble. Sex may temporarily give you the impression that everything is better because it instantly boosts your levels of all the feel-good chemicals. Sexual intimacy might lead you to assume that you and your partner are emotionally closer than you are. But in the end, it can't resolve significant problems. Do you then turn to sex to solve your problems?

1 You have flings intermittently;

If you use sex to solve issues, then every time you have adversity in life (what do I want to be when I grow up? How do we mend this split in our family?) You've started a brand-new, intense affair. Flings may entirely take your mind off of your worries since they are often all-immersive and focused only on sex. But as soon as you have to deal with those problems, you become disinterested in your romance.

2 You convert sober discussions into sexual relations;

You feel awkward if your spouse wants to speak to you about a relationship issue. As the talk progresses, you normally start cracking jokes a lot and ultimately move on to more sexual topics.

3 Sadness often makes you feel horny;
Sadness is closely followed by horniness. The Pavlov's dogs experiment was performed on you. Your body has gotten used to creating sex hormones the instant you experience melancholy because you use sex so often to escape from misery.

4 Rarely are you horny while you're really happy;
Do you know how when you're depressed you become horny? You haven't needed to

have sex throughout extended periods when you haven't faced a significant life challenge. When you're content, you like to spend time with friends, travel, and engage in activities outside of the bedroom. This can also be a result of the conditioning your brain has received. Your mind is aware that it must make the most of your current state of happiness since if you're sad once again, it will just be sex.

Chapter 4

Facets of a relationship other than sex:

A young guy gives his lover a passionate kiss on the forehead, making her grin broadly. The quality of your covert behaviors is less significant for the long-term success of your relationship than feeling emotionally safe in it.

A relationship's need for sex is not universal, and experts contend that other aspects may be more important.

You may become more intimate with one another via quality time, emotional safety, and other sorts of closeness.

If you often experience sexual unfulfillment, expressing your wants in a relaxed, honest dialogue may be helpful.
Every partnership is different. Therefore, although some couples may prioritize having sex, others may place a higher value on other relationship-related factors.

There are several reasons why partners may not prioritize sex.

For instance, having less sex desire, being asexual, foregoing sex out of respect for one's culture or religion, or having specific medical issues, might all be contributing factors.

Happiness in a relationship is not just dependent on sexual activity. It isn't necessarily a must for a satisfying relationship, however.

In fact, according to specialists, the following related factors could even be more significant than sexual activity.

1. Feeling secure

Emotional safety is the cornerstone of every loving and supportive relationship.

You must feel emotionally secure to be open and vulnerable with your lover.

For instance, you should feel comfortable discussing your concerns with your spouse without worrying about their response if you feel ignored by them or if something they said hurts you.

Contrarily, partners who don't feel emotionally comfortable may react defensively or aggressively during arguments and retreat, shut down, or completely avoid confrontation.

These actions may obstruct communication and, in certain situations, foster hidden resentments.

Developing emotional security might involve:

Inform them when something they do irritates you, but do it without accusing them so they understand you are giving them the benefit of the doubt.
Summarize or reflect on what they said to demonstrate that you have heard them and are interested in their ideas and emotions.
By expressing empathy and validating their feelings, you can: That would have been very stressful, therefore it makes natural that you would feel sad in that circumstance. I'd have the same emotions.

2. Personalized time

Spending time with your spouse, whether it be simply chatting or engaging in an activity, may benefit you in the following ways:

Feel more content in your relationship.
Recognize more good aspects of your union
Feel more intimate with your lover.
The amount of time you should spend together is not subject to any strict guidelines. Finding what works for you is ultimately what's important, according to experts. This may mean scheduling a date night once a week, setting out an hour each day, or scheduling a stretch of bonding time on the weekends.

Shared experiences are effective because they may reveal points of commonality. They may also inspire you to keep advancing the relationship and give you a sense of unity, teamwork, and happy memories.

A couple will feel more bonded if they can take time out from their busy days to be there for one another.

3. Complementary interactions

Marriages tend to last longer when there are at least five good encounters for every bad one.

Negative interactions might involve shouting at your spouse or ignoring their emotions, as well as giving them quiet treatment. The closeness, respect, and trust in your relationship may suffer as a result of these actions.

On the other hand, you may engage in more fruitful relationships via maintaining eye contact, asking open-ended questions, and engaging in contemplative listening.

You may demonstrate your sincere interest in your partner's remarks.

Hugging them when they get home from work, giving them a back massage while you watch a movie, or holding their hand while you walk around the neighborhood are all ways to show physical love.

Gratitude and appreciation for the things they do to make your life simpler should be expressed along with compliments.
Instead of concentrating only on your disagreements, try to find areas of agreement when you are in dispute.
Expressing genuine apologies after doing anything offensive.
During conversations and small arguments, try to find ways to laugh together to reduce tension and brighten the atmosphere.

4. Closeness

A feeling of intimacy fosters a sense of intimacy. Many people believe that intimacy exclusively refers to having sex, however, physical closeness is merely one aspect.

Other forms of closeness that are as significant include:

Intellectual or mental closeness includes sharing new information. You may consider taking a cooking class together or talking about interesting subjects that interest both of you.

Emotional closeness entails sharing your deepest wishes, worries, and ideas. By asking open-ended queries such as, "What makes you feel the most loved?" you might inspire your spouse to express their feelings in the same way. "What is anything you want to do but are afraid to do?" or "What is the greatest thing I can do for you when you're stressed?"

Interpersonal intimacy: This might refer to any kind of cooperation. You may discover a shared pastime or take on home repair tasks together to foster this form of connection.

5. Respect

Respect for one another in a relationship may encourage more openness and vulnerability as well as emotions of security and trust. Even better relationship pleasure and quality may result from it.

In regular contact, respect may be shown via regard for limits,
allowing each other room as necessary,
assisting one another's objectives and interests.
Recognizing each other as distinct people with their wants and goals.

The antithesis of respect, and contempt, may weaken your relationship. In summary, failing to treat your spouse with respect may undermine their sense of worth and cause them to become dissatisfied, unhappy, or even indifferent.

Physical closeness is important, too.
The consensus among experts is that not all partnerships need sex. Many individuals may keep happy relationships going by concentrating on closeness in other areas.

Remember that physical closeness does not solely include sex. Holding hands, snuggling, embracing, and kissing might help you maintain a physical connection. All of these physical interactions can cause the release of oxytocin, a hormone known to have a substantial bonding function, much like sex.

More frequent kissing was associated with better relationship quality in a 2013 research, but surprisingly, individuals who responded to an online questionnaire did not identify the same association when it came to the frequency of sex.

In addition, partners who engaged in more non-sexual physical touch tended to be happier in their relationships, according to a 2020 research on heterosexual married couples.

In the end, what matters most is that both you and your spouse are content. Put your attention on developing closeness in other areas if your sex requirements and wants are out of sync.

The main goal of sex, is to make people feel connected. Your sex desire may be affected if one of you doesn't feel that way.

What to do if you don't like the way sex is done in your relationship:

To explore any underlying problems or concerns affecting your sex life, its ideal to see a relationship counselor or sex therapist.

A sex therapist may also provide advice on how to express your partner's sexual demands to them.

Pressuring versus asking

Informing your lover that you want to have sex more often is never inappropriate. Just be careful not to coerce them into having sex if they don't want to since compulsion and sexual pressure are indications of abuse.

If you feel comfortable doing so, you may try telling them how the pressure makes you feel if they continue to attempt to convince you to have sex after you've previously said no.

Its advisable that if you don't feel satisfied in your sex life, you must tell your spouse. Given that this is a delicate consider the following suggestions:

Pick a moment that's not stressful. In other words, discuss it while they are at home on a lazy Sunday afternoon rather than just before they go for an appointment or just after they get home after a busy day at work. Start by using consoling language. Starting the discussion with something positive, such as, rather than making allegations that can put them on the defensive "I'm currently incredibly content with several aspects of our relationship, including [X, Y, and Z]. However, one thing I'd want to work on with you is physical closeness."

Come with a sense of wonder. Try expressing observations and asking questions instead of declaring things like, "We don't have enough sex," such as, "I've noticed we haven't been having sex as often as we used to and I'm curious: Why do you think that is?"

Although it may be a potent means of establishing and maintaining intimacy, sex is not strictly necessary for a relationship to succeed.

One is that there are several non-sexual techniques to encourage physical closeness in a relationship. But you could even discover that giving other aspects of your relationship more importance, such as respect, emotional stability, quality time, constructive communication, and general closeness, can do much to make your connection stronger.

Having said that, experts concur that you should feel comfortable discussing your unhappiness with your spouse in a cool, honest, and non judgmental manner if you and your partner have very different sexual requirements.

Chapter 5

Strategies to Save Relationship Problems / issues:

1.RelationshipIssue Communication:

All communication issues are the root cause of all relationship issues.
You cannot converse while checking your BlackBerry, watching TV, or reading the sports section.

Approaches to tackling communication issues;

Make a scheduled appointment

Put the children to bed, put the mobile phones on vibrate, and let voicemail take your calls if you share a house.

If you find it difficult to "communicate" without yelling, choose a public area such as a park, library, or restaurant where you won't feel ashamed if anybody overhears you.

Set some guidelines.
Try to wait until your spouse has finished speaking before interjecting, or avoid saying something like "You always..." or "You never..."

Display your listening by using your body language.
Don't fiddle with your nails, glance at your watch, or doodle.
If necessary, reword your response and nod to let the other person know you understand.

Say something like, "I hear you stating that even though we both work, you feel like you have more tasks at home."
The other can verify if you're correct.
You may state it in a friendlier manner if what the other person wanted to say was, "Hey, you're a slob and you make extra work for me by having to clean up after you."

Plan everything.
Scheduling a time, but not necessarily late at night when everyone is exhausted.
Perhaps during the infant's Saturday afternoon sleep or a "quickie before work."

Every other Friday night, ask friends or relatives to take the youngsters to a sleepover.
When sex is scheduled, you get more eager.
She argues that a little variety may also increase the enjoyment of sex.
Why not engage in sexual activity there?
maybe by the fire?
or when erect in the hallway?

Creating a personal "Sexy List" for each of you to discover what genuinely makes you and your spouse hot.
Swap the lists to come up with additional situations that will make you both happy.

Speaking with a licensed sex therapist to help you confront and resolve your difficulties if your sexual relationship problems can't be managed on your own.

2. Relationship Issue: Finances

Even before the wedding vows are exchanged, money issues might arise.
They may result, for instance, from the high price of a wedding or from the costs associated with wooing.
Couples who are having financial difficulties must take a deep breath and have an honest discussion about money matters.

Approaches to tackling Finances issues;

Tell the truth about your financial standing right now.
Maintaining the same lifestyle after circumstances have become worse is impractical.

Avoid addressing the issue while the fight is still going on.
Instead, choose a time that works for both of you and is not frightening.

Accept the possibility that one spouse is a spender and the other a saver, realize there are advantages to both, and resolve to profit from each other's habits.

Never conceal money or debt.
Bring financial records to the table, such as a current credit report, pay stubs, bank accounts, insurance policies, debt statements, and investment statements.

Place no blame.

Create a shared budget that accounts for savings.

Choose who will be in charge of making monthly bill payments.

By allocating funds that may be used as they see fit, you can give each individual the freedom to be independent.

Set both immediate and long-term objectives.
Individual objectives are OK, but you should also have family aspirations.

Discuss how to take care of your parents as they age and, if necessary, how to properly arrange for their financial requirements.

3. Relationship Issue: Conflict Over Household Tasks

The majority of partners have jobs outside the house, sometimes several jobs. It's crucial to evenly share the work at home.

Approaches to tackling household tasks issues;

Being orderly and clear about your responsibilities at home.
"List all the tasks and decide who is responsible for each"
Be fair so that anger doesn't fester.

Consider other options.
Consider hiring a cleaning service if you and your partner detest doing the dishes.
The other spouse may take care of the laundry and the yard if one of you enjoys doing the chores.
You may use your imagination and consider preferences as long as it seems equitable to both of you.

4. Relationship Issue: Not Prioritizing Your Relationship

Making your relationship the center of attention shouldn't stop after you say "I do" if you want to keep your romantic life continuing.
Relationships become less exciting.
Decide to prioritize yours, find it, hold onto it, and make it endure.

Approaches to tackling not prioritizing your relationship issues;

Make the same moves you did when you first started dating:
Communicate with one another throughout the day, express gratitude, and offer compliments.

Schedule dating evenings.
Just as you would for any other significant event in your life, block out time for your relationship on the calendar.

Show each other respect.
Thank you and please know that I appreciate it.
It conveys to your spouse that they are important.

5. Relationship issue: Conflict in Relationships

Sometimes disagreement is a natural aspect of life.
But if you and your spouse feel like you and the movie Groundhog Day are playing out the same terrible scenarios over and over again, it's time to break out of this destructive pattern.
When you put in the effort, you may lower your level of rage and examine the root causes of the problem calmly.

Approaches to tackling conflict in relationships issues;

Your spouse may learn to disagree in a more respectful, constructive way.
Integrate these tactics into your persona in this connection.

Understand that you are not a victim.
You have the decision of whether and how to respond.

Be truthful to yourself.
Are your words intended to end the disagreement or are you seeking retaliation while you're engaged in an argument?
It's advisable to take a moment to breathe deeply and alter your course if your statements are accusatory and harsh.

Variate it.
You cannot anticipate a different outcome this time if you continue to act in the same

manner that has caused you grief and sorrow in the past.
A little adjustment alone may have a significant impact.
Hold out for a few seconds if you often speak up to defend yourself before your spouse has done speaking.
You'll be astonished at how a tiny adjustment in speed can completely alter the tone of a discussion.

Give little to get much.
When you're incorrect, apologize.
Yes, it's challenging, but give it a go and marvel at the results.

The conduct of others is beyond your control, Silverman asserts.
You are the sole one under your authority.

6. Relationship Issue: Lack of trust

The foundation of every relationship is trust.

Do some things you see make you doubt your partner?
Or are you unable to trust people because of unsolved issues?

Approaches to tackling issues;

By using these suggestions, you and your spouse may build confidence in one another.

- Be dependable.
- Be punctual.
- Follow through on your promises.
- Never lie to your lover or anybody else, not even small white lies.
- Even while you are arguing, be fair.
- Respect the sentiments of the other person.
- Although you may still argue, be mindful of your partner's emotions.
- When you say you will call, do call.
-
- Tell them you'll be arriving late via phone.

- Take on a good amount of labor.
- When things go wrong, try not to overreact.
- Never make statements that you cannot retract.
- Try not to reopen past wounds.
- Honor the limits set by your spouse.
- Be not envious.
- Take time to listen.

Chapter 6

Conclusion

Even though there will always be issues in a relationship, you and your partner may take steps to lessen or even completely prevent marital issues.

Be practical first. It's a Hollywood dream to believe your partner will take care of all your wants and be able to anticipate them. Ask directly for what you need, she advises.

Use humor next to help people relax and appreciate one another more.

Last but not least, be prepared to improve your relationship and honestly assess what has to be done.
Don't assume that having someone else would make things better. No matter what kind of relationship you're in, problems will continue to arise if you don't address the issues that are now causing them.

When couples use sex to patch things up after arguments, they often discover that it did not take away the disappointment or

annoyance they were experiencing. They only had a brief respite as a result.
Sex also cannot take the place of authentic remorse for wrongdoing. Your difficulties are still there after you're done, despite how nice it feels. Couples gradually realize that using sex to resolve conflicts isn't as beneficial to their marriage as they had believed.

It seems sensible to want to reevaluate a relationship when one or both partners have strayed.
However, having sex too soon after adultery is discovered might make things more difficult. Sexual activity is enjoyable and produces hormones that strengthen the sense of intimacy. It is probably ineffective to use it to "patch up" a relationship when the problems are concealed or not spoken about.

The likelihood is great that the excitement of sex and the rekindling of a romantic connection may obscure the reasons why the affair took place, lulling one or both partners into a false feeling of security. For instance, a couple may believe that everything is well since they have had a passion and that forgiving has been effective. The adultery victim could be left simmering with a variety of feelings after the excitement has died down, from rage and resentment to self-loathing.

The same is true in cases of abuse. Giving into sex with a partner who is verbally, emotionally, or even physically violent may make the victim feel betrayed and hated for themselves. Even if it may be appreciated in the heat of the moment, sex may turn into an adversary that devalues and undermines the abused partner's sense of self-preservation, leaving such people feeling helpless and betrayed by their bodies.

Intervention is unquestionably required in these cases since sex may contribute to the cycle of abuse.

Sex may turn into an escape rather than addressing the pressing problems at hand, even in other situations when verbal communication may be weak in the marriage. Either partner may use the sexual expression as a distraction technique in place of expressing and talking about issues. When we are coerced in this manner, we could comply only to maintain the peace without actually addressing the annoying problem.

While I don't advocate delaying a couple's sexual life until everything is ideal, it's important to understand that relationships have many facets. Yes, sex indeed receives a lot of attention, as is to be anticipated. However, it's as crucial to be conscious of the underlying problems that influence all of our conduct, including our sexual activity.

We might remain in a sexual rut due to problems like fear, poor communication, codependency, and even victim mentality. As a result, the person or couple continues to develop slowly, and their sex life never develops into the liberating force that it was intended to be. Victim-based sex might detract from the relationship's worth rather than add to it. Undoubtedly, to address the root of a problem, external assistance may be necessary, thus this alternative should be considered. It is advisable to seek the help of a counselor or a therapist.

Our relationships need to be connected if they are to succeed, just as our lives need to be integrated if we are to feel whole and at peace. While our sexual connection does serve to define marriage and set it apart from other types of relationships, it is not the primary component. Sex cannot be the answer to every issue in relationship since it has many facets.

On the other hand, fantastic, ecstatic sex does not guarantee that a couple's relationship is on solid ground. But it is considerably more powerful to use that sexual connection to cultivate and show selfless love. Since sex is what it is if a couple craves that connection in any circumstance, at least their desire may be utilized as the catalyst to start the conversation.

www.ingramcontent.com/pod-product-compliance
Lightning Source LLC
LaVergne TN
LVHW020525160826
845677LV00015B/3915
9798356688409